# Listen. If

# Listen. If

Douglas Barbour

 THE UNIVERSITY
*of* ALBERTA PRESS

Published by

**The University of Alberta Press**
Ring House 2
Edmonton, Alberta, Canada  T6G 2E1
www.uap.ualberta.ca

Library and Archives Canada Cataloguing in Publication

Barbour, Douglas, 1940-, author
Listen. If / Douglas Barbour.

(Robert Kroetsch series)
Issued in print and electronic formats.
ISBN 978-1-77212-254-1 (softcover).—
ISBN 978-1-77212-307-4 (PDF)

I. Title.  II. Series: Robert Kroetsch series

PS8555.A76L57 2017        C811'.54        C2016-907991-0
                          C2016-907992-9


First edition, first printing, 2017.
First printed and bound in Canada by Houghton Boston Printers,
Saskatoon, Saskatchewan.
Copyediting and proofreading by Peter Midgley

A volume in the Robert Kroetsch Series.

The University of Alberta Press is committed to protecting our natural environment.
As part of our efforts, this book is printed on Enviro Paper:
it contains 100% post-consumer recycled fibres and is acid- and chlorine-free.

The University of Alberta Press gratefully acknowledges the support received for its
publishing program from the Government of Canada, the Canada Council for the Arts,
and the Government of Alberta through the Alberta Media Fund.

For Sharon
　　　Another fifty years


in the light　no gloom
　　gathering　but bright
　　　sounds　the conversation

growing　all these years
　　together　to gather
　　　here　friends

family　a long time
　　we all have something
　　　to say to each other

# Contents

Listen. If I have known beauty
let's say I came to it
asking

—PHYLLIS WEBB

Acts of Memory

## Robert & Robert

'the river is quiet
                    unperturbed'

it is    it was
the oyster sticks laid down
just below the waterline

sun  or moon
light laid along that smooth
surface

'my double loves touch me
                        very simply'

their words
across the Hawkesbury
or San Francisco Bay

Robert & Robert    singing
a catch

phrase     phase
of the tune

# 2 for Robert Creeley

**i**

I wanted to
to get there

to get into
the words turned
as if on a lathe

of heaven sent
stutter fall
the way they
took the breath

right out of me

he was older than when
that near shout of
for Christ's sake

got my attention
& got my attention
with words that turned
on a sense of aging
wisdom

how to get there
where I might be
now   now I inhale

the same unstale
air he told us we
all must breathe

some
time

**ii**
only once met him, heard him
knowing that extended moment
was in the presence of what
measure spoke
of smallest motions
what that audience as
one knew with him   then
could carry into night

I remember what I dont remember. A dream of memory or so it seemed. Seems. To be a memory of what I couldnt remember except in dreams, those stories of stories untold. That I was there with other students, married friends when only youthful lovers before I knew them, coming out of that house full of music I heard so much about later. Me on the lawn waving    & in that dream aware that this is the past & I'm in it. That past Ive only heard of from others. Me then in that memory, lost.

The sunshine laid upon the land
signed spring or fall
I couldnt tell which

# 'dilution of memory'

ghosts it seems
    or just grave corpses

bones of an army
    gone to rust and sand

'troops and kit...
    pretty frayed at the edges'

how edgy then
    and now   inturned

to ward off memory
    pay no attention

crumpled hills of metal
    left for remembrance

flowers of offal
    'all fall down'

# VE Day

memory twists & resists across all those years yet this one has always
it seems been there as i always remember it the same way or is it
the story it's become in my mind that somehow stays the same
as i look up at my mother standing there a shadowy silhouette
above me dark against new bright light streaming through
the window now she'd raised the blinds (always down
for years now? always?   that i cannot remember)
telling me this is such a great day   dougie
the war is over isn't that a great thing?

that bright red dot
in the southern sky here

memories encoded

those first bounding steps
my mother reminded me
I had spoken of when very young

she standing in kitchen
unbelieving / yet
we watched together
those leaps in black & white
on TV
        (soon to thrust further
to the nearest planet

for sure

& the years gather
            rather
reports on executive failures
even the space station
slowly sinking
while the aging shuttles
& imagination
sit on the tarmac
downed

# fifty years modality

so kind
of new then
                now too
blue blues
        sing bruising
                song line
lost in silences so
        rhythmically held

all these years
        for ears
                still here

# a bit of a trip

that voice   ethereal
soaring   wafted
into elevator
rising   in some
small hotel   in
some small city
in what used
to be east germany
constant  &  craving
we rise too

Seasonals

# Autumn

'We don't write about autumn,
we write about fall. We have
fall here and not very much of it.'

—ROBERT KROETSCH

fall fell far too soon
this year

yet today's sun has
    fallen only so far
        down the bright
            blue sky

& the trees their
leaves unfallen colour
full in 'the white of
    dazzling light' a
            -chieves

'a transparent light of
        meaning'  for a
moment  &  moving

across valley
    walls a cast
        sudden
glowing quilt

'no self here
        to find, no
                proper name'

left

leaves on the street  to
pedal through yellow   sheer sere
sun lower in sky


gutter leaves
curb leaves
leaves shards
left braided
across concrete

leaves leaving
branches behind
a kind
of lofty
loss   leaves
empty branches
stark   as
lief to go


bracketed by puddles
the leaf-carpeted path
stretches brightly off

the fresh clear water
also strewn
with glowing orange
& umber leaves

& among that colour
full glitter   reflections
of slim trunks    dark sky
a sudden susurrus
& a few more drift slowly down

zero morning
sun bright   slant
on river   lead   on
leaves bronze & gold
stretched along the valley

runners   heavy breath
floats up   white
behind them
pale moon
fading on the arras
of blue


I think I'll go
put on a parka
throw my hands in the air
& whine

or an anorak
for the rain
now falling  perhaps

in Britain


toward Rocky Mountain House

the prairies roll
fields lift & fall
in long slow waves
we create driving through

grey ribbon of road
stretches down & away
arrow straight till it rises
once more into a tunnel of trees

the fields   shades of brown
bundled   turned black earth
trees a tartan   evergreen
yellow  tawny    suddenly bright

across this horizon tall space
traced by sun & cloud
a human geometry emerges

# Winter

first snow  falling slow
hangs in the air
a curtain drifting there
thickening sight

you see
either the depth of
the lines of   or
certain flakes shifting
immediate  then
twisting   & gone

while slowly the trees
& houses fade
away    into
a distance    made only
of white descent

as night
          gently falls
into place


waiting for the sun
remember half
a world away
waiting for the sun

to shine on hot sand
not reflect off
cold white snow

the sound the same
a gritty squeak
from heavy boots
or bare feet

when from Arctic corridors
wind's enforced passage
in snow's sustained

a whiteout wrestles
across embattled wastes
forests overturn

trees ripped untimely
in sudden frost
shine aslant   thrown down

weather or whither
such losses gain
a roll call of what's gone

gathers    clouds
on an interior horizon
never measured


stark woodcut
branches emerge
sudden beneath
street lights


an absolute chill
    clarity of air

pastel sky        pale
    blue   falls toward
        an almost unseen green
      orange gauze   darkling pink
the black crouch of low hill beyond the river

above god
s pared fingernail
    hangs there
    tossed aside

indifferent

to all tidal twists
& turns below


that only brown grass scuffed to dirt
hammers each sole that descends
no matter how carefully while in
pain the breath scatters in white
clouds above the slowly moving
few snivelling toward home



lawn & street white    thick
with new snow    hung
in bare branches   &
hunched in the heavy
evergreen needles

beyond   the sky
grey almost to white
then caught in a glimpse
only   wing flash of blue
black   lifts angular

out of shovelled blind
across garage corner
to what landing above
& out of sight

the blue through the bell tower
beckons &
          fades inwards
enclosed as heaven held fast
while all around more blue
hastens outward pale
shadows shift
their possibilities
across the snow
so whitely blued below


a winter sky
          so clear
a single breath
          smudges the stars


full moon casts onto
a skiff of snow  shadows
of barren branches


take that icy blue
          made darker
                    warmer
in the shadowy footsteps
          across the snow

so early in the morning
          so late at night
winter's stories    told
          again    step by  step

a haze hangs
across the city

a snow fall
s low pall

bells would crack
tolled in such cold

breath short
white in the air

the city's exhaust
ion

# Spring

what season is it

       against a dull metal sky
            huge white flakes   float
                    down as leaves might
            some months hence
       such cool beauty    dissipating


greenflare
buds burn bright
against the blue

emerald dark
will come
beyond transparent
openings   a glow
arriving soon


on that cusp
a moment only
green grows the
buds break out
a parchment in
scribed by photo
synthesis now so
transparently open to
what will come


up north here but
a few days allow
this transformation

how the aspens lined
along the river bluff
mellow guardians

blanched tall standards
bare but not
barren begin

to float in
transparent green
gauze of new

ly unfurling leaf
buds thinly flexing
on the unruined choirs

in just one week a
filigree of leaves covers
the river valley

as always now
the river valley
fills with green
                 light
glisters in
the burgeoning leaves
falling in waves
                 up
the surrounding bluffs

catching up   as
usual clouds
sun       interact

flickers in furze
soar     or

eyes catch leafturn
something as fast as
a breath
            that car there
passing


leaf buds
trees bristle


caught once again in that long hesitation
                (greening gestation    until leaves open

this quickly gone transparency
            coming    it seems
                more quickly    each year

a turn    return
        so unlike the new change
            of perspective

each single vote constructed


Leaves

trans
lucent    let be

lated    come into
    greening as rain
        falls    the occasional

parent   purify
    colour so thin
    it slow   it grow
    it darken now
    beyond snow

ference   how mind
    mends as it moves beyond

position
    that the world
    goes on despite
    & as

cendant   to blight
    what's

left

# Summer

semper empirical
the return each year
transcends pessimism

first phantoms of
other springs arrive
in their translucence

something new derive
a newest green
transitory gleam

as the trans sports
into fuller summer


against the scarves
of drifting cloud
& slowly dimming light

the cranes appear
stark    sigils
of steel tower

above new poured concrete
stiles   stand attentive
against the still bright dusk

the calligraphy
of clouds / plane signs its name in
invisible ink

or the Cézanne lines
below / a geometry
blue green and fading

into the eye's grasp
on paper or canvas / those
shattered surfaces

some walls harbour more
light fractaled on flat entrance
meant denying depth

The Age Demanding

cranes stand at ease
above the works   the works
stand still
all grab attention


you are above it all   for to
fly in such a machined manner
over a world not fully formatted
Canada's empty spaces   the
north especially   though
it's shrinking   the ice caps once
so pristine & massive
pretty much gone to ocean now


the first move involves
truth gone down   this
is every day's lesson    what
replaced knowledge
by any other name is
silence   a mute
and blinded acquiescence   just
the way things are
silence remains
is all we would know
a palliative
lie for all

# a ghazal for the angry old man

wheelchaired Gore Vidal at 84   remains
angry   knows as always   skeleton keys

The Republican Party is not a political party.
It's a mindset, like Hitler Youth.

all that hatred in this or that closet
a closed mind betrays a body

rye and gingerly wry
and gender bent

& the slow secret hurricane
government sponsored   damage controlled


you shall know them     then
by the funerals they keep
the companies they find there
the cold stare
                        the dead
hand of ideology
handed on
carved into stone


a penchant for war
forewarned is
four armed
forces

gone into the dark

a pen chants for peace
for warned is
for ward
ing off

look toward the light


watched the man lie
again   move as if
on strings

mouth words
once meaningful
demeaned by misuse

lay that wreath
those crocodile tears
a slow march

never learned
in the real
just the bought

and sanitized
all that quick march
sans the lonely dead


is the world still with us
at all    the planet turns
beneath us impersonal

but not unperturbed
by how the world's
waning law lost

in the snow or sand
ploughed through
exploded   the idea

thrown out against
that heatdeath of
the mind mined

and blown up out
of proportion
all the freedom

promised and denied
the world spins
its own narrative thread


the body in tatters
flayed
          displayed

in Baghdad
Karbala
Port au Prince
          deployed

the flails of safe belief
fall
the whips of scorn

no body left
to right

'My God how the money flows in'

the brand new bright blue gates to the city of Babylon originals
museumed in Berlin hang askew in the rockets' red glare where
are the little goddesses light encased once but gone walkabout
with thieves as Hammurabi and Saddam looked on askance
from the perch in the painted clouds of their muraled eternal
presence incapable of anything more than silent acquiescence
such robbery once the prerogative of kings only only now the
rabble rouse to emulation as beside the dried out riverbed
who weeps for a green garden lost forever in the blown dust
of explosives machine guns the blade in the chinks of stone

Babylon's blue gates
gone down what goddesses dance
for life and love now


just one
just one child
just one child dead
just one child dead   just
just one child dead   just one
just one child dead   just one   just

ice in the eye of
such beholders hold
ing such power   all
righteous mess all
gone down as

just one child dead
lies there   demonstrating
lies there


take away
heresy then hearsay
evidence becomes a

wandering gesture
away with words
yes to say

ought to / go
figure what

time to get to
heaven I'm in
even token

war renders the
overlord beyond
reform / laying down
law lawlessly
denies the ground stood upon

'there is a lot of ruin
      in a nation'

so much beyond this dark
night sky
            white ground
held together by
      the slow fall
      ing snow flakes
            their silence
      a veil & reproach

before the gathering ruin
      in so many nations
            silence alone

no voice
      as ever before death

singular    or
improbably beyond counting

a few bent notes
                    blue
hover still
     in the bleak air


cries to heaven:
question. mark.

cries to heaven:
questions. marked.

sighs unleavened yet
unquestioning. marketed

lies to sever
questions. mark.


is only one death
numinous    no

mention of but one
even as so
many others die in
other places   & do none
remember them   or
inflect remorse
as if before death all
memories reach equally out


Mounting then a defense   but
against what   why
have one ordinary Canadian
even if born in Syria   so
removed & so sequestered (for that year)

All international legalities lost in a kind of
revenge it seems /   this latest war
against abstraction while the person
rendered overseas turns non


what worlds float
fragmented        washed astray
into   & through
lenses      held  apart

a necessary distance

oil slicks on a northern lake
blue  & rainbowed
& sluicing across
a sunburnt arm down south

so a city     streets of
river   bursting
through first storey windows

the broken
the lost
the gone

silence  only
a rhetoric sufficient to

the washed away

We are in charge here   so
don't mess with us     We can
eavesdrop on anyone anytime
enough of them are found
on no solid ground
the law we ignored in
secret no longer counts    whole
conversations captured
among those we know as enemy

things ain't what they used to be


Then the 'Babylonians themselves say
owing to the great size of the city

the outskirts were captured
without the people in the centre

knowing anything
about it'   But 'Babylon

was now doomed
to destruction'

and now these words & the ruins
they celebrate are but craters

in sand stretched far away
walls fallen in then & elsewhere

but others new built
beyond that rusty horizon

where some prepare to cull
the usual suspects

a stain of war
black   sludging
along the pebbled
shore     roar
to spread   north
darkling   as from
above   the only certitude
grows more confused
with each tide

## Double haiku for a damaged world

Don't read those headlines
the thin moon grins   grimaces
Think of my dead dust

On a blasted plain
a single cherry blossom
drifts on a grey breeze


'i' 'saw'
3? ships
'come' 'sailing'
where?

in time or space
connected as if to

3 ships ply
Gulf waters
guns alert

& long before
3 sails waft
before the wind
trading
    news

& someday
circling that
planet earthly

3 ships seed
hope before
war tears

the fabric
the veil
the faith
to sail


& so died a myriad
      not well done    that
so many   undone by plans
      to save     thus
they must suffer     so much
      destruction    fell
falling   white nacre
      from the unforgiving sky

It's over is it over

Love's Fragmented Narrative

**1**

*Love hurts        love scars*
thats how you know it
s love                care
full        it can break
you        know it

for the love
ly  pain
it con
tains


**2**

*Round and round   up we go*
a song of highs
& lows

    o yeah   we
say        we go down
too        its some
fucking ride

## 3

*So youre stretched out in room 1009*
loves a drug      you
know better than
to take alone

      or do you

now    'stretched out'    strung out
feel like youre falling        for days

'in love'

## 4

*Every night          every day*
the same pain    &        other
wise      feeling

OK  OK

i asked for it          i
got it          good

## 5

*Want to know if the fishing boats coming*
in yet          yeah
there it is

ooh  someones          looking good
                              out there     &
in a few hours    more

even better      in
here

## 6

*Mama  leave the front door open tonight*
who used to say      used to
say that every night                    now

'i' got my own keys          own
door
          keep it open    please

come in
love

# 7

*Sun goes down on a sultry day*
nights sultry too     or
i am

          come on     lets
make love     weve got
the whole sultry night     &
i want you

# 8

*Maggie was a lady*
look where that got her

     no          lets be workers
lets get beyond that

     for love

## 9

Dont lead me on
'like' nothing id care to talk about

just dont        eh

just come here now

## 10

Standing in the doorway
well        make up yr mind

like the song says
either come or go
quietly
        & slow
if you stay        coming
in

## 11

*The first thing that dies*
should be the memory

its not

oh   god   damn   you

its not


## 12

*Look at who the winds blowing up the road*
right past my door

       thats how i want to sing it

right past my door
keep going     now
ive almost forgotten
how to open it

to you

## 13

*Dont make me over*
again

      it was  too
difficult    last time

like making beauty
then
hiding it in a cave

too difficult    by half

## 14

*They say no one can call on you*
especially when in need

i dont want to
call on you

tell you im in need

## 15

*Sign on the window says lonely*

it always does
damned signification

now  youre gone

## 16

*There are words to say*
everything
              if you know them

thats what they say
they say the words are there
to say        but all i say

   please
   give me the right
   words  for
   once

## 17

*I hear your voice in my ear*

i *hear*
it    dont
want to    cant
help it

want to    / help
me    forget

## 18

*We were walking in the sand*
holding hands    i bet

loving every silly
minute of it        unaware

it was    quick
sand        how
sunk i was
in goddamned    you

## 19

*Would I kid you now*

well    id try anything
to finally
get you out of my life

& good riddance
finally

would i kid you about that

## 20

*Let us pause in life's pleasures*
few as i find them      yet
more each day

it i pause to reflect
its to say        OK
im  OK  im
OK        pleasures
of the day
suffice & grow

you gone

Trans —

## sit the deer

deer's silence
thicket of grass
thick stems of brush
of insects   buzz   & ears
listening
for those other sounds

sit there
the deer / silent
& slowly going in
to that space   alone   there

sky bright   blue
everywhere smudged
white fluffs   move   quick
shadows in the grass

beyond   the trees
heavy slabs of   browns   greens
& the sly animal
movements you listen for
in there   under the thick
vegetable roof   listen
for danger

go in
to yr silence
a peace
there   you sit
the deer   quiet
the wind   whispers
peace   for the moment   for
this time   go in

to the thicket
lie down

be
the deer's
silence    be
there

# Rose

*for/from Alan Loney*


breaking flat tide

bent pier
          dark     dark

learn slowness

cloud gliding

high     forgotten face

even diffuse
          non-reflective almost
rooftops below rain

pleasure upon high

hanging
          dragged along

hawk just waiting

forwarding procession
          looking

changing

digging out mud

here
          tears

illuminate

tufts winds rippled

small wake

small wide-awake craft

kingfisher
          evening's

fierce high
drifting flares

what cry

of detritus
circles invisible boundaries
scattering direction

wind buffeting
hits

harbour
boat shimmering
discontinuous gold

inhabiting solitude
a landscape step

raw horizon

day lights clouds
underneath

dazzling patches
random cloud

alive

moon's exactly sun

tender

pair recall
hearing all

says delight

walking with humans

wherever

cloud over love
frayed edges of

enduring
life  death

flaring off

## Roses / Blue
*(an arbitrary choosing from ED Blodgett)*


flesh hypothesis all
    every walk upon I    you
    when children skin upon hands
we rose to air
    have may about all than more
the into    the of    their fall
    might skies but be
    be cannot through drift
    they perhaps air bright I

us the of that choreography us between
    other as their of beginnings
no that words that see and saw the air their of
    and spoke but and
    (were nymphs stories of their measuring
the with    the across it
    (bride all past   coming

ground almost rose invisible
    rise upon rain
    gaze eyes through falls stars
    those no have
    are why against unseen
    to about the on of symmetry
    but themselves that in all

rain would they surrender
    a their within we
    see us give ourselves offering complete
contain for longing  growing stone
their   from been    have beyond we and mind
    image
one the of we
as the of a
    air the on a
    within we

day remembered rain surprise
the but rain    could I
        and mortality
into rise the be and solitude receding
        suns was he    the when
        upon stood the saw my


Mouth beside
        radiate the speak it sky
        flesh become I
        rose reply
continuous might anyone burning above
        surrounds that is breath
        enfold to its of inchoate still I


hands there    horizons
what became of  unsure of     endlessness
        to enough  because we transfigured skies
with memories came deaths
        our beside the
        see upon hand  dimly
        ritual when


memory  that stones can
        we a anywhere   his within possession
        our the
        near our of
        an us   of fires
        the what your upon  as sight
        alphabets becoming     think


now becoming yours
        a more the within knowing earth
        you our
        upon their
and you perhaps so lies within
        frail to remains
        eternity one beneath bones
        this

down    and grass to need
    purple fall
have you white falling
    and rain        the

mouth fountains
    sky desire
    and of anemones the on the
    in the against the
if the immersed what say I
    flesh sometimes
    and remember not serenities luxuriant
    fish    flesh   and opulent I

# Triptych for an angry fall

### 1.

They are the enemy & we know they are   we
said realistic expectations  all-out effort   will not end
Here we take our stand  launching  indefinitely   what
are reconfirmed   moderate to severe damage   to
the terrorists everywhere against our good will   These
maps explain everything  including which tyrants
we have to support to save democracy   A
burned chador or hospital is only
the usual collateral damage  In their
cities they will come to understand this  In ours they already do

### 2.

The US initiative, they all spoke of
razing shepherds' houses, said to fight terrorism,
to take a stand   Here is my body
politic   always they are suspected Islamic rebels
planting bombs on the streets of 'our'
cities   Look, the maps do not lie
Only four hundred, we have the guns
You have been burned by negotiations again
and to exchange the land of god
to have safe cities is not enough

### 3.

'Serbian policemen' or 'the Yugoslav army'? they
seem effectively intimidating either way  Whose pixilated face said
compliance is not a reality & who cares?  Here
& now dug into the hills opposite shivering nights & days are
alive with the sound of mortars, the missile's song, the
euphemism working for whose greater glory?  Our maps
still say Sarajevo too, not to mention Kosovo, 600 years old but we
know better, the buildings not blasted are burned
& not a single roof remains to keep the
snow & ice from filling in the empty holes of the cities

# Tucson sallies:

**1a)**
No building or square so quiet
weapons won't wreak havoc there. What's
allowed in Tucson is more than I
in Edmonton ever knew. Even the
Library of Congress is 'armed.'

**1b)**
The churches & temples in all names insist their
gods are the one. A desert will
do that to people, & in Tucson what's
not desert is not much. You might
subtract the churches outside town
from those within & still have more than a
man's faith can sustain. Yet they're
allotted space, buildings beside the mountains,
time to bring such messages as they can to
the people waiting for
hours in the hot sun to receive blessings. 'I
spent a week there one day
in stubborn heat oppressed. Whoever was
fishing for my soul used the wrong bait.'

**2a)**
No wonder we keep
weapons at a distance. What is & is not
allowed beside the central square
in Tucson I don't know. A whole
library probably couldn't explain it quite.

**2b)**

The mountains surround the city like distant
gods observing a huge game board. What they
do upon it felt there whether or
not they exist. Try to
subtract the desert sands
from the towering rocks they say build
man's necessary temples on their
allotted sites. In St. John of the Wilderness it's
time to pray & eat
the locusts of disregard. How many
hours of meditation have you
spent emptying the self
in patient abnegation almost like
fishing with your father all those years ago.

**3a)**

No place so lovely, in Tucson Arizona,
weapons of all kinds are not
allowed. Most effective
in the long run, however,
library books invade another mind.

# The Ten Steps of Zen

### 1

Looking everywhere's a mistake
for getting there    you must leave
the field,  the woods, & seek the
bull where it's already pawing the sand

### 2

Discovering then your fear you will put
the story of its failure            & the
bull's success behind you,    nothing but
footsteps across hoofprints—calm & undisturbed

### 3

Discovering anything            especially
the outlines of the known
bull is always difficult

### 4

Catching it harder      &
the outcome is unknown to you if not the
bull      whose motivation is suspect anyway

### 5

Taming it might change
the logic of the search          but the
bull is under no obligation  there

**6**

Riding off in all directions is
the wrong answer      a
bull knows but one way
home & you must not try to guide it

**7**

The end of this
bull ride is both home
transcended & entered—found perhaps

**8**

The bull was an absence      or image of the
Self      as you always suspected.      What
transcended possibility can you seek now

**9**

Returning seems impossible now you've gotten
to this point    yet it's
the only way you'll ever find the
source of all this struggle

**10**

In every koan there's only
the desire to put you back in the
world where you always were                anyway

civilization        has its version of
primal scattering   languages
                    riddle via metaphor
                        linguistic chaos
   Pandora's box

A lunatic tower
      broken
          like Tantalus
            lost all
            of myth

          The history of
               *illuminati*
     is itself      compelling
          turgid
          baroque torsions
                              focussed
                the metaphoric
             touch
             emblematic
                                  Babel
will feel
        celestial motion
                amazed
          estrangement from
          language
  deeps of
                debate
shallower ground

It is not                    past
    It is
                         Images                                              past
    Imprinted                                                           on our
                              era
active                  past or          past
                                      regress or
               past    echoes
the reach                           of
                    mechanisms
                    of continuity
         Where
                    a long interval of
                         grammar                                    is
created by
                         'history'
         modern
         metaphysical
vestiges
         were          almost
         the natural
                    religion
         individual
         intimations
                                        dark and sacred

    which man    had
against    natural                 being

# up there, yes, up there

**i**

everlasting flows reflecting splendour
thought waters feeble
mountains   waterfalls   contend ceaselessly

**ii**

dark vale
       and awful Power
from these   thou giant children come

mighty solemn rainbows veil strange voices
       eternity echoing loud motion

that gaze sublime
my mind receives
       an universe of darkness
       where still shadows
            are faint recalls

**iii**

remoter death shapes those unknown

          I dream inaccessibly
             spirit driven among the snowy mountains
             broad unfathomable heaven

accumulated storms   eagle
wolf    and ghastly Earthquake-daemon
       were silent now

wilderness teaches man faith
Mountain understood by feel

**iv**

the living lightning   earthquake dreams

      dreamless the trance
      of all that revolve apart
      remote       naked

               I teach snakes on scorn

piled city of ruin
boundaries vast mangled stand
waste world never becomes
their lost dwelling

      Vanish place
      shine from
      majestic blood
      loud circling

**v**

power of sounds
calm the mountain

burn through snow
rapid   voiceless   and sweet

thought inhabits earth
                    human
      silence

# The Gap

'the gap, from which all things emerge'

—SHARON THESEN


or into which all falls
     fulfills history's provenance
       'a legal black hole'
     filling up with 'houses of parliament,
         giants, stones'   or
         giant stones   upon which
            carved words slowly crumble


craters gap disbelief
as wind wafts across destruction
     blows detritus into eyes

sandstorm   ashstorm
     flakes of bodies torn

what wings tremble above
this latest pileup   grates
     grows greater
     bodies crushed inside

engines still ticking

(where'd you get that file
     ditch it

cornucopia  or  abyss
        does it open
                close
       is there a tiny light
                  ahead

foreseen       forsworn
       huge atriums
           caverns of delight
       opening
           sales


or better yet      bardo
      latry        labrys
turning on a threshold
caught upon the in-between
      gulf  Brownian

      whose sense of reality
      whose confrontation with the real
          carved into curving time


Lacan's   lacunae
      speech fettered    faltered
         into psyche's holes
         memory's losses
            (intended?
     that they alter
       'native' possibilities

& if the soul be empty
     words hollow out
     meaning dissipates on the wind


gap   gap   gap   gape
gawp   gawp       gasp

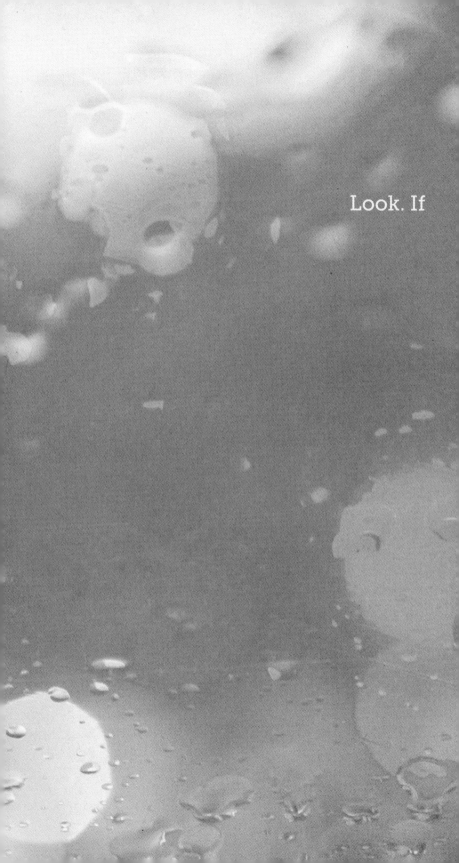

Look. If

## Cézanne's last years

& he moved    he
moved    through paint
& canvas stretched after canvas
towards a simplicity

so complex it
simply takes our eyes
                              out
& then    in        there

sketches    the
sketches    of a place
a world he knew
& renewed
on the canvas
of what he saw
how he saw it

blocks of colour   of
light    of
the bare canvas    the bare
page

fewer gestures
say more
he says
in his language

& i repeat
repeat it
in mine

# Claude Monet:  'Les Nympheas'

to enter in  /  to
the light    /
            colours
of the queen of all
                   life

light

       the surface     vast
       contains

it all
light    colour     the forms
of earth alive

              surface chaotic
he painted  /
           centred

look    it
pulls perception in

we enter

the light

      (homage to the world

         & vision        vision
      expanding
          through   failing flesh
            to felt             joy

the canvas
barely contains

the flowers

light

everywhere

# homage à Claude Monet

**1**
the light
        floats!
in a small pond

in the streams       streams
                    of light

      altar

the paintings   all
         turned

                      utterly

**2**
lilies    the

water / lilies

            afloat

in    light

**3**
arbour

           (h)   arbour

       *au bout de la*

               *lumière*

light
ly

# utamaro's women

the frame of the mirror & the sash of her kimono mesh to frame her
face     the space between     & her face    facing away     facing her own
face in the mirror mirroring one quick delicate act in what moment
stolen

she fingers her hair in the mirror      her stare from the mirror
rests on her hair hidden by her head her fingers tease a hair into
place     she had placed herself before the mirror the better to see her
hair     misplaced so     she reaches to tease it back      into place     this
place allows her a mirror where she can stare back & forth    at her
misplaced hair there it is in place now     what are the two pairs of
eyes staring at

So Matisse       you bring me
here     this line of
people massing to see

what             what
paint can do
disposed by eye & hand
across one canvas
                          then another
then another
                    mais  c'est Paris
ces coleurs brillants
                          they always
grab me

        red     & blue      &

# Tom Thomson: 'The Jack Pine' 1916–1917

If no ones present presence presents a vertical
movement the absent i partakes of sky *spreading*
(thats *not* sprawl all gone into the world of light or
dark hills hiding the just folks he paddled away from
every chance he got reds deep blues seize the day / light
slowly its taken 70 years now fading over the water
the leaves colour theres that rock at the bottom of
everything were supposed to pay no attention &
away away the lone line leaps beyond the frame up
toward the sky he you i drowned in is that ice
ice or only a reflection the reception of that gone
time hand moving on the waters continues

THE NATIONAL GALLERY, OTTAWA

# for/from David Milne

**1**

a transparency of
                        houses
                lines in white of

of winter        distancing

the steps taken            across
            the field
                    of light
                            green        running


it 'takes' 'you'        that
many years to
        stumble
                    through shadings *vert*
vertiginous
the thick brush of
        those colours
                sliding

all the way
        in        out        to:


**2**

how a colour colours the surround & how the paper flushes green
purple that red there that line how the smallest detail
is part of a pattern is growing outward & utterly flat on
that paper or canvas that gentian  lake  rock   those signs
already signalling surrender to the palette  a plateful of
harvest  snow  water reflecting the above all of the
painter painting 'it' down on to into a form from
which the eye cannot be drawn  drawn in  intimate
smallness expanding outward to & beyond the borders
of the frame up to whatever heaven colours come from

it was an eye
               saw it
     a hand
             moved   it

is the thing itself

             paint
                   on
                         canvas


there—

**3**
when north
train stayed summer

different or far place
old tent settled

moved from reasonable distance
time painted waterlilies
captured in bottles

the waterlilies were excuse

diffuse  light

# homage à roy kiyooka
*(his StoneDGloveS)*
*in memoriam*

and on the snow bound street
one hand holds the tire rut—

rotting glove.

# elegiac
*i.m. syd barrett*

Come into the light
on something else again lost
you throw you away
stranger to those songs

you gone beyond those bright lights
legend fallen in

you thunder    you howl
martyr thrust from melody
and in your own dark
shine on

# Jack Chambers:  'Nude 74-76'

it is an empty room     it is
the artist's studio     it is    not
empty    the presence of the young woman
fills it    the artist
present too    and perhaps
we are present in the aery spaces of the empty room

there is a radiator along the left side wall    a
radiator along the back wall    they are very
straight & the edges of the floor are clear
the windows high to the young woman's right
almost glow    they are white    they are the light
floating into the room    the back wall is there
you can see the wall sockets    the paint
swathed on in testing for colour    a paper
stuck onto the wall    it is
there    not there /    (where)
he has painted the air    solid
& fleeting like time    the woman
who stands there    to stare    out at    us

the wall fades    the linoleum shifts
beneath her feet    in /
substantial    the lunar landing site    bright
in space /    the earth parched & waiting
for rain    & again    there is presence
a light    & delight in the forms
she is there    she is body
bodying forth
all the life he can see    he can paint
what he sees    what he sees
is much more
than at first we would know
of a young woman naked
alone in a large sunlit room where the walls
open out to the cosmos

& she stands with her body
a system of brush strokes    a series of planes
curves of muscle    of flesh

the painting refuses
to hold all in place
yet places each element
all four held together
all contraries gathered
                        that light
in the body
            that body
in the light

as the room    & the artist
& the woman    within
hustle thru space
to the time of the stars
to the time of
            the eye
which has seen
                & expressed
in the pigments & patinas
of oil on canvas
that all this once was

& it opens    it
opens    the wall
is so solid
yet the corner dissolves
into light    solid
light
        & the mind
of the painter    his sight
his delight
is    all there
with the woman
who stands    & is solid
as present    as human
in    a space    that is only
a room    full of space
those boundless bounds opening

## for Barbara Caruso (i.m.)

such clean lines
clear    the colours
so contained    so
constructed    construed
the mind that thought
those complements
felt them too

those colours
gone  now
into the dark


always a geometry to it
   the basics first    then
      a bit skewed     slowly
         colours on the bias

till finally fractaled
   those made colours
      slid into place
         accompanying one another

& ever smaller fragments touched
   on the cuts      parts
      of blue    or green    horizons


that she alone
   mixed the colours
      squeezing each tube

then   on white    that loss
    or black     that dark
        substrata


how each small touch of
    underpaint / innerpaint
        darkening  or lightening

backed the new tone of
    toward some sought after
        realm    now seen clear

# floating head songs

At last they killed you and broke you in pieces while
your sound kept lingering on in lions and boulders.
in trees and in birds. There you are singing still.

— RAINER MARIA RILKE,
*The Sonnets to Orpheus*,
TRANSLATED BY STEPHEN MICHELL

a

              float
oats
      seed in

time

                 rime

             (the snows

fall

the head floats
           free

at last of
love
           (the prison house of

                    beyond

sing        sing

the hills beyond                              the hills beyond
                              &
                    rush        (rusts)
                 where the river run


                    seen from this perspective
                         & approached thus


the stone head                    left behind
            sings secrets

Or what the ploughman didnt notice

                                 that time

        a splash        legs high

                           or
              a head         hair
                 lost in waves

singing
the song would have drawn him off &

                                away

long
     gone
         song

of every rock & rill
echoing from every hill

      loss
      tossed
      upon the waves

whirling
        ahead

    sings past
        loss


the dark tunnel
    her shining face      fading

all those women    tearing
    across gradually green slopes

        meat
        just
        ice
        I
        chanted
        for
        th
            floating

a darkening blue

a cast of heavy rose

     the hills green shadow

                    ahead in the water

                         last light glints


    spreading to
              the sea

ahead
            the sea


sate

            you are

# Recording Dates

In to & out of
your mind again      you're on your
own again     catching all the sweat &
sweet taste of a single moment    single
way of putting your mouth on skin or metal        now

# May 15 1953

Perdido: memory gone. That's how it works. You
salt the mind, still hoping for the real. They got
peanuts for the gig but you got the memory.
All the way back to 1953 and what
the hell happened that night. Those nights. There are some
things you only know by hearsay, yet it's that story
you heard about ten years later & read about. Those few hours
are part of your memory now—as if you'd been there, listening.
Wee? No it was huge    cool or
hot it doesn't matter, they tore the
house down for a small crowd soon to grow with telling.
A wonderful feeling, watching that white plastic wave & weave all
night long & the notes pour forth. Heaven-pointed trumpet, everyone
in synch: great music for the ages & you can still hear A Night in
Tunisia every time you place the disc just so.

# May 15 1953

Perdido          but nothing's ever      they may
salt the fields  someone wrote it down / someone got it on tape   the
                                                    Intro to Salt
Peanuts as 'my worthy constituent' took up his horn &
all the breath he needed        & then blew
the highest notes you'd ever heard. There are some
things we are meant to know          to hear.   The tale told over &
                                                    over &
you read it too        ten years later          those few hours
are part of your memory now, your secret history:        thousands
                                                    listening into the
wee small hours as five musicians from somewhere else made
hot music hotter   & faster   & more brilliant    till the
house lights came on   & the audience was too small for the stories
                                                    later.
A listener weeps now with frustration wanting to believe the
night was that full    that more of the citizens
in strait-laced Toronto knew their greatness & wanted to hear A
                                                    Night in
Tunisia & other classics to be          to be there   to be hearing it
                                                    (again (now

# October 26 1956

It means something more than
never stepping into the same note twice  They
entered & enter still a space made of sound but still
my heart feels blues notes we were paid no never
mind to focusing attention wholly through them to
four ways of being precisely there
in the breath & the melody made now in
your mind listening & playing both  You
own it & let it go knowing with
sweet abandon each note is
way beyond possession & even leaving
the stand's a way of taking a stand  That
theme runs through every improvised solo & now
Trane's rushing up & down scales where angels fear to trace the
blues tells all tells nothing  How it got there gathering shards of
Ahmad's story or Miles's story or all their stories are just the
blues writ large against the backdrop of white America
Half a continent drenched in it that they can't hear in
Nelson or Salt Lake City or even New York City sometimes
the stark & bitter news of a cabaret card taken becomes a
theme for another lengthy solo & the silence it bares

# December 1961–November 1962

Say it was a beginning then
it was an ending too  always
over and over again the one
and the other play through the melodies played
over till they're known in the body once
again as fresh as the first time loved still

You hear them fresh then now
don't you you play them with such ease you
know the inner structure intimate
what you'll take apart in a
love so supreme you'll make it whole someday
is that what you're beginning to realize

Too far too soon the roar of the
young lion's a growl smeared
to shatter structure of easy come easy
go away into sounds barriers broken yet a
steady running beat of blood sustains the wail

All of the sounds gather in your head
or everything comes to
nothing if you can't push it out
at the world pushing back
all that ecstasy so loud & melodic it moves

I humbly asked to be given the means and
wish to reach the point of making music spirit and now
I do perceive and have been duly re-informed of what I
knew all along these secular songs only suggest

It's going to come he finds it
easy to hear the future in these popular invitations
to the profanest dance I now
remember is holy holy holy too

Nancy where are you are words
with little meaning for him yet
the poem appeared about the same time as they were
laughing listening to the playbacks of songs for her for anyone would
face the music & what it portends

# November 15 1957

All right   all night   into the
mornin' sun casting
long shadows across the studio's floor
they watched them shorten   We
can't remember or understand how one
take 17 minutes long works   but
that is what they were there for   Take
away the bottles, ashtrays,
from then to now's a short step for
me   for you   for whoever's listening
our will to do so is the shared
delight they made possible,  making music as always

# May 23 1963

Scrapple sliced & fried a long way
from New York  you have to make
the stuff in a small kitchen   still life
apple & orange on the wooden table
willow or oak it'd make you
weep to think where it came from
for whom it was originally built why
me in Paris so far from
Broadway yet in 1963 a
stairway up from &
to some kind of ordinary acceptance
the citizens back home still refused so many
stars   in music  dance  art  writing
a way away from
night knew no innocence
in Harlem growing up  listening to rhythms
Tunisia started, or Morocco, the Congo all
our ancestors weaving a form of
love in drumbeats & sliding notes   a voice
is raised on high to cry
here I am  here is the way
to clamber up these steps
stay where at least they listen
like they care to hear
someone make a joyous new world noise
in Paris in a studio together in
love with the sound all over again

# October 9 & 10 1974

Death behind or before this chord
and that one interchangeable then
the final sounding  expansive  horn of a
flower or dilemma opening into night all contra in a
prayer so profound or far away how
great to open sky through which the last
bird spreads its wings & soars beyond the moon

Death comes in many guises, a black bird
and a white whale equally partake of the great,
the intense and final prayer,
flower of the atom, atomy of the flower.
Prayer is both response to and refusal of the
great journey now begun, whale and
bird both taking the shortest route possible to death.

# March 2 1953

These are the days,  nothing so
foolish as making music       Some
things are forever,  or at least to
remind you of one night when for
me now as you four then all
of it was right    The music played
you,  you played
Perdido, something by Hoagy, say
Stardust,  & a few other well known tunes.
The band was cooking in the
way it could but
you know it wasn't always like this.
Look,  listen,  learn once again that
tonight is only tonight &
how you reached that recorded summit
high above the average gig when
the music simply poured forth  & the
moon seemed to lean down through that window to listen

# June 15 1961

My fingered thoughts on being
foolish take shape here,  an inscribed
heart or mind: to be read      But this
waltz,  that ballad,  a whole, popular history played
for us,   how America sang throughout this blood-drenched century.
Debbie or Mark or Greg or Sandy know nothing,  they
detour around history,  then run smack into it
ahead   The music will out, & the dead still making it on
my stereo:  that's the real
romance of time technologic.
Some days it is enough
Other nights there're the ur notes to keep
time keep time away   One of the
milestones of my life was hearing him play
Porgy  but for the small fact
I never did      Music
loves to mess with memory that way.
You know       the time you saw
Porgy and Bess,        or was that
Gloria's story,   a
step away from whom when
my lies or memories are any
man's  & the event's long
gone anyway         I write it
now as truth and fiction   while
solar flares fuck the reception &
Alice doesn't play here anymore     For one moment
in time that club was a
wonderland where
all three players got it right  And
of death to come they knew less than even
you as you read,  or me,  the subtle
jade statue of past & present
visions caught on tape & reprogrammed simply by us all

## July 1977

Peace is what we're here
for, a time out of time  when
five men take a
3/4 beat   & swing it gently
in a pristine German studio.
The music made that
afternoon gentles my soul
sumother time & time again   each
song a song for whoever listens.
Deer prance across the far lawn beneath a
wan moon fading over the lake

# July 26 1974

Antibes is the place,  all right.
What can we do about it    What
is there to do in
this paradise but our
thing    Play something old
called jazz,  play something new,  and
love emerges with every honked note.
Round here everyone cares
about music,  morning, noon, well after
midnight someone's playing somewhere.
You're sure to find
a jam session there,  become another
weaver of melodies,  the lost & found notes
of songs remembered,  or invented in
dreams & brought suddenly into
the light,  or the night,  that
song is you now,
is yours to change each time
you take a breath to blow spring or
autumn,  summer or winter,  the music
leaves seasons reasons behind & just is.

# June 26 1957

Abide   abode   aubade   abundant
with strange sounds  although to
me they make perfect sense    You too?
Well, that's how it should be   &
you know it    What's needed
needn't stop anyone from grabbing for the
ruby even if they miss    I told
my brother he'd regret borrowing so
dear   They'll break his arms
off anyway if he doesn't pay up   A
minor nuisance, hardly worth the bother.
Epistrophy's the name for every payment   Nightly.
Crepescule the time of darkness descending
with money due again   Whoa
Nellie, you can't escape   We want it now.

# September 10 1994

Introduction to the groove    Her
Equinox balances sun & moon    Notes float above
Berkshire hills,  the leaves trill, a
Blues thrill,  fingers can only move that fast
if you're preternaturally gifted
I would say,  but I know nothing  & you
were playing with
a tough but gentle swing, the toll of a distant
bell or the siren around
the corner, or someone's cry    Use a
Sheik in sex or music:
wrap something protective between
your heart & each note as it
troubles the living stream
in & out of
dreams constructing aural purity    Who's to
say it doesn't work    Who's to say
it won't    You play the same notes
over & over again
and they're not the same    Then it's
over till the next time    Once
again it's time you've defeated &
we listen,  close our eyes  &
see the possibilities.

# January 12 1956

I was 16 in Montréal & you'd never
guess who my friends were  anyway
I'll tell you all I knew of jazz wouldn't
have filled a single notebook page   I want
to go back to that long ago &
change things so the world then matches
my nostalgic eclectic dreaming   How else
plan to be somewhere these cats were playing.

I'd wish to have heard them live but
didn't even know their names then,  didn't
know that music   it wasn't
what I heard on the radio   At that
time we listened to The Hit Parade:
it wasn't even real rock & roll yet
was just something striving for muzak without realizing it.

Gigantic figures in their world of mostly unheard
blues they played America even if most refused to hear.

This was 'the jazz life' & one
year's records or gigs floated away a memory of
kisses & as hard to recall once the lips are gone.

You know it too  & whether opera or jazz we
can only receive its gifts when we no longer
depend on them   Or anyone needs them ? Put
on your high heeled sneakers,  dance with
me to the end of these brand new old tunes.

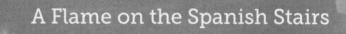
A Flame on the Spanish Stairs

I know now I always wanted to write, to
find a way to release the dreams
that spelled desire onto the page
I loved letters from the first for what they
cannot hide—their own palimpsests they
exist in multiple layers of time
without even thinking about it that is what
poetry means to me now     &
without desire nothing's written but          death
eternal to keep us apart.   Oh, there must be
poetry to remember beauty by   & for me at least
half that beauty is your body          flush with
the soul within   but never mine to hold
day or night you are but imagination's grace


at least that's how it seems   coughing the
last of my breath redly out in
the backstreets of Rome      then the very
idea that we could have shared our bodies
has an air of desperate folly  I have
grown much worse lately     & I dream
so much of you          yet I grow
monstrously weak    only my imagination soars
beyond the mundane details of
my slowly approaching death          all is a
seeming        & there you glow        the
power of your body,  your eyes & smile
of welcome once      now lost to all
attainment      —        only my heart still wishes

a way of going the song says & I think it a
test of my memory as well as
of my love    Charles would accuse me of too much
invention  & he may be right        I want that
which I can never have      & so
I rave & write & think to somehow
take back enough time
to marry      it would
be my greatest delight to lead you to
the marriage bed at last      not lie in
polar sheets so far from the single
star I seek      oh yes I can write myths
of gods & goddesses but the moon knows it's only
poetry          another page of lies


I am lost darling girl & I
cannot even write to you to
express my desire    not just
how I want to make love to you but how
I so desperately need your love too      Do not
despise me please    these thoughts
the fever brings but they are truth  the
man not the poet speaking  seeking
who else but love herself in you
would you not forgive that
wrong if wrong desire be    but it isn't either/
or now with me        autumn will
be my goddess now  & she knows how
impertinent spring had to be

the books of my peers shine with the light of
imagination   & I am glad I lived to read them      It
may be I will never match them      but to
be known as one who tried will suffice
compared to Shakespeare we must all admit
to a stature so small as to have been overlooked in
Adam's garden          As in a
dream we will pass from memory & only
he will remain,   ever greater                    I
awoke from a dream of the moon
and I knew I had
found my subject       then I wrote
it down in hundreds of lines &
truth be known I was sick to heart at my failure




girl      you come to me
in fever dreams now while
soldiers stand guard & you shed your
clothes bright with purpose how often I have
wished to see you in an unguarded moment
she at least could come to me last night   &
had a message
only for my eyes       It has
been hard enduring such
a slow dying          No
man should have to suffer that
for anything    but
Tom's listening & will say nothing for the
sake of my heart

memory is a hard mistress   strange that I
should see all processes as feminine now
not that it probably isn't so  I would
be a fool to dismiss the messages imagination
called me to now      It's a kind of
knowledge I'd rather not have but
many I know
have met it in their time & in this I'm not
original        Mortality clears all
minds when it says once more
who do you think you are
do not try to escape me       I am
not what you
think but neither am I not


great thoughts don't you think    what a
pity I will never know if
that is what
people wanted from a dying youth   I
should have lived       &
by your leave with you        my darling
associating with the great poets
themselves as much in love
with you as I   & knowing
the pleasure I took in your
finest love       a pure delight in all
things  letting nothing
spoil the days & years we spent with
them on the slopes of Parnassus

the vision I have from here is that
disfigurement of civil grace
I know others have also seen          I
mean what poets must legislate against
is that so much to ask                    that
the imagination know the
miasma of the real      cities
of greed & avarice Blake saw in
London          a cesspool
I consider will
do well as symbol of what I
suppose my congested lungs also signify
it has to do with the human
contaminated by grief & anger but also love

the way I feel now a
poet is a sad thing indeed     he
has nothing to show for his efforts &
none will pay him      attention
no      he loses his
identity yet identifies with everything
he loves          & much he does not    It
is a wonder he even remembers words &
certainly he finds them at
the wrong moment
most are charlatans despite all       only the truly
unpoetical have any hope
of doing anything worthwhile at
all       (if they're lucky)

kiss kiss   kiss kiss     I would inform
them all that
that verb is the only one
I want to hear from you       It
may be indiscreet to say so but
at most I alone will know & at
least I know now that your
touch is all I really wanted
my dreams of your
lips on mine, on me
where it would not matter   & mine on
yours everywhere I worship                I
have dreamed this     & then have
been awakened to be bled once more

to wake each morning now &
brood about my losses     love
over & done with       & me still
in boyhood knowing
my constitution will keep me there till death
walks with you along
your favourite paths  reflecting in your
loveliness my joy
and desire       that is
the dream I cherish each
hour I still breathe     is it so foolish
of me to dream so       It is
my only small joy in the face of the
death I also see in my handkerchief each morning

die is what I will do soon      but never
content to do so while separated from
and lost to
my desired love      All my
friends will live on &
should they feel sorrow will
drink to my memory & together raise
a toast to poems unwritten   If I'm lucky about a
dozen will gather sometimes to think
of their old friend & what I never knew      A fine
claret will serve         &
on that day each year they'll read one of
my poems & throw flowers on my
tomb to dry in days to come




the death I know so intimately claims
more of me each day
I weep shamelessly & wish to
have a good dying      but I have
known too many bad ones    Oh love
you are well away from this & from
the lust my fever brings      The
more I remember chaste embraces the more
I wish they had not been so  I
have had enough of chastity & I
loved you well beyond propriety
in my dreaming body dying
every night alas the
way was blocked by rules & we're lost

my heart is broken & my
dear girl is lost forever
Shelley will tell all     but
I will be lost in the allegory
am I that much the ghost already
very well then            it doesn't
much matter what I really felt & I'm
gratified to know he will care
that the poet died alone in Rome
you will know the lover
in his thrall fell far too fast due to
a lack of breath   spirit   in this
foreign city sans language love the
country I desire still


the dreams I have now are sweetest
persuasion to die quickly
that is all
I have left to do
shall I bemoan that I shall never
see you again        my goddess moon in
her changes shone not half so bright
no you have visited me these nights &
more though you
will never know      It would
kill me again if you found that out about
me     Rather my poems tell you how much
I loved you     purely as I
cannot tell you now

# Acknowledgements

Thanks to Sheila Murphy, who read the first draft & made some
excellent editorial suggestions. Thanks to Peter Midgley, for
asking the right questions, & the rest of the crew at University of
Alberta Press, Alan, Cathie, & Monika.

I'm grateful to the editors of the following journals, who
published many of these poems: *Canadian Poetries* (online),
*dANDelion, filling station, The Literary Review of Canada,
Jacket* (online), *Pacific Poetries* (online), *The Peter F Yacht Club,
poetryetc* (online).

One of the Keats sonnets appeared in *In Fine Form* (eds.
Kate Braid & Sandy Shreve. Polestar 2005). "Tom Thomson:
'The Jack Pine' 1916-1917" & "utamaro's women" appeared in
*Threshold: An Anthology of Contemporary Writing from Alberta*
(ed. Srdja Pavlovic. University of Alberta Press, 1999). Some
of these poems appeared in *Wednesdays'* (above/ground press,
2008) & in *Vision/Sounding* (The League of Canadian Poets).
"up there, yes, up there" was first published by housepress.

*It's over is it over* appeared as an above/ground chapbook
in 2005; *A Flame on the Spanish Stairs* was published by
greenboathousebooks in 2002; *Recording Dates* was published
by Rubicon Press in 2012. My thanks to rob mclennan, Jason
Dewinetz, & Jenna Butler.